deanna—

Israel's friend —

& my friend

i love you & i

believe in Jesus

rom. 12:1

"It's Incredible!"

ANN KIEMEL "It's

Incredible!

Tyndale House Publishers, Inc.
Wheaton, Illinois

Library of Congress Catalog Card Number 77-072443
ISBN 0-8423-1820-8, cloth
Copyright © 1977 by Tyndale House Publishers, Inc.,
    Wheaton, Illinois. All rights reserved.
First printing, June 1977
Printed in the United States of America

to three men who have brought
great love and joy to me—

fred, my brother
tom, my brother-in-law
thomas eugene ream, III, my nephew

contents

Jan and Ann admire Jan's new son Thomas Eugene Ream, III.

to my twin sister

11   jan,
you are my favorite
person in the
whole world.
you make me laugh hard
and feel whole
and strong and vibrant
and needed. you add
dignity to life...
peace, love.

you notice my clothes and hair
and ideas and dreams
when no one else seems
to.

you cook gourmet dishes with
mushrooms and seasonings and unknown
spices. you dress your walls with
design and warmth. you
have a great husband, and even
he says you are wonderful.
you are fine and beautiful
and decisive and individualistic.

someday, i hope we can write names
in the sunset, and ride bikes
for hours, and rise early to care for
healthy babies. someday
i hope we have big fireplaces
in old homes, and families that
create and laugh and share and
love and dream.

12   God gave me you...
and you have made so much difference.
jan, my great person.
i love you.

the long haul

13   when i was a small girl, my father would say,
        "ann, it pays to serve Jesus...."
    i would respond,
        "why, daddy...? i am nine years old, and
           ugly, and hardly anyone likes me."

    and he'd smile, and tousle my hair, and say,
    "GIVE GOD TIME...."

give God time.
i wish it were simple ... i wish that patience
    had been born in my
        heart and mind and veins.

the LONG HAUL is what really matters.
today, i am thirty, and i can say,
    "daddy, you were right ... Jesus has
        changed the color of EVERYTHING."

but between nine and thirty, there was a lot of
working, and a huge amount of waiting. from the
time i was in grade school, clear through high school, i
didn't feel very special or accepted by anyone but my
family.
    there were many days i went to school with no
    one to pat me on the back ... no one to applaud
    me or care what i dreamed.

    for years i tried to throw my best into common
    days. the college years when i dragged through
    the snow to the cafeteria to work my way
    through. the classes that weren't easy or were so
    dull that i forced myself to go again and again
    and again. the times i wished i had a date with

14   someone extraordinary,
          and didn't.

the two years of teaching school, i was terribly poor,
  and very lonely. my friend jeanne millhuff was my
    one ray of color ... but i remember getting into
      my little car and sobbing through the streets
        of kansas city. i had thought if i could get
          through college, and out into the REAL
          world, life would be tremendous.
        but there were so many crooked corners
          and gaps out there.

of course, from the time i was a youth director in
california, through my years as dean of women at
eastern nazarene college outside boston, i had so
many mistakes to make...
    so many flaws to be shown up...
      so many lessons to learn and
        battles to fight.

i had days when everyone seemed to love me, and
days when it seemed hardly anyone did.

often, when i've flown out-of-town to address a
convention, people will say, "oh, they must love you at
the college."
    and i laugh and say,
    "well ... some of them don't even like me."
    smile.

the LONG HAUL...
it's taken all those years combined
to make me what i am today.

15   to mellow me.
        to smooth the rough edges.
        to reveal my true colors.

        EVERYBODY dreams.
        no one has ever been born without dreams.
        the wino sitting on the curb carries dreams.
        the long haul divides the stouthearted
           from the halfhearted...
              it shows who is willing to pay the price,
                 and who isn't....
              it levels everything, and reveals the truth.

        my friend paul miller says life is sort of like a
        cauldron. put all the people and experiences into it,
        and while they are learning to work together,
           while there are disagreements and
              misunderstandings...
              no one can tell exactly what the truth is.
        but give it time to simmer and cook, and when the
        stirring stops, TRUTH will rise to the surface. there
        may be a lot of buffeting and criticism and opposition,
        but in time, what is right will come to the top.

        i've boarded airplanes to go speak somewhere,
        when i had no courage at all.
        just sheer, gut determination to tell
        my story, and want others to dream, too.
        there have been lots of layovers in cold airports, when
        i've found a telephone booth to hide in, and have
        cried and cried.

        i am an everyday young woman.
           not an extraordinary beauty.

16   not a fireball of talent.
it's taken years of "homework" to get my dreams
communicated. years and years of trying to help
people believe that they and a great God can move
their worlds.

i've been tagged a "pollyanna" and "unrealistic"
but i've pressed on ... convinced that
    God's love can create a hole in ANY mountain, leap
        every barrier, if given time.

recently, i spoke to a group at west point academy. a
school car and driver took me back to the airport to
come home.
    the driver was a young, handsome black, and we
    began to talk. he told how he'd been paralyzed
    from the waist down ... was flat on his back for
    months ... finally, the doctor operated and
    removed a tumor on his spine.
he had to teach his brain all over again how to send
signals to his arms and legs. finally, after long periods
of time in hospitals far from home and family, the
doctor came in and said,
    "robert, if you can walk from here to physical
        therapy, you can go home for awhile...."

robert tried to describe to me how painful it was.
that all through the hospital corridors, he kept saying,
"i can't go on ... it hurts too bad. i've
    got to quit."

then he'd think of his two children
and his family, and he would keep pushing. no one
was there to support him...

just a dream in his mind...
and after three hours, he collapsed at the door
of physical therapy, and the doctor was standing
there to congratulate him.

the long haul reveals who's telling the truth
        and who isn't...
    whether the criticisms about you and me from
        others are valid or invalid.
    whose hearts are pure and whose aren't.
the long haul always surfaces what we've sown.

i want time to reveal that
i've done my best...
    that Jesus has found me trustworthy...
that every day is sobering and exciting.
my race isn't finished yet.

it's INCREDIBLE...
it means i can believe that EVERY day
    every ounce of effort
        every gesture of love
will SOME day make ALL the difference.

some of you may feel the long haul hasn't
made a difference yet ... hasn't paid off.
i know a boy named lloyd, and he said i could tell you
some pieces about his life...
he's twenty years old.
he says,
"i really missed my parents when i was young. i don't
ever remember my mother being at home. she was
always working. my first memory is of getting up
while it was still dark, packing a suitcase full of toys,

18   and going to a cranky old babysitter who must have
hated kids. an orphanage would have been better
because at least there would have been a feeling of
community. even her cat was
        very nervous, and hated kids ... and
        my parents never paid much attention to how
other kids dressed or wore their hair. my hair
was always about as long as telly savalas', but
nobody ever heard of him, then.
        my clothes were always three for a dollar from
the dime store. my babysitters treated me like a
disease to be kept away from their kids. IF
ANYBODY SAYS HE FEELS REJECTED, I
CAN SAY I UNDERSTAND.

        "coming from rejection into puberty, i didn't
have much of a chance. my three-for-a-dollar
clothes and my homestyle haircut didn't help
much. getting into a fist fight would have helped
my self-image, but i was too inhibited for that. i
needed to feel masculine, but i didn't know
how..."

it has been a LONG haul for lloyd...
        but Jesus is helping him.
            he's learning to build relationships
                and to like himself.

lloyd,
i'm proud of you.
your road has been a lot harder than mine.
you're brave and determined,
and in time, that will change EVERYTHING.

19   lloyd once said,
      "ann, there are a lot of losses
          for every important gain...."

      wherever you are,
      don't let the losses drag you down.
      Jesus is running with you, and He'll pool
      it all into a great moment
      some day.

my family

21   my father is, as my brother would say, a
"Bible-thumping" preacher. mother says he's
preaching louder than ever, but people seem to love
it...
and so do i.

he married my mother after traveling 'most the world
over in evangelism. she was a kansas schoolteacher
and had been a child prodigy in piano. to me she was
always a sophisticated, beautiful lady,
    but when she married my dad, she
    invested her whole life in him and us...
    as we came along.

rather than playing in concert halls, my mom would
sit at the piano and ramble from "tea for two" to a
little jazz and our favorite hymns. she played in all the
churches where my dad pastored. everyone loved
her.

some preachers get nice parsonages, but we never
did. ours were usually pretty old, and poorly painted,
and i well remember jan and me crying.

    "you girls, wait 'til i'm finished with this house.
    you'll love it. why, no one will ever know it's the
    same one...."

she was right.
we came to love dearly every parsonage we lived
in ... even the first one in hawaii with the
bedrooms at one end of the sanctuary, and the
kitchen at the other. our bathrooms were the
"men's" and "ladies'" at the church. the termites

dug little holes in the walls of our rooms, and
        swarmed over the lights at mealtime ... but there
        was so much love and laughter, and pretty colors
        and curtains, that we didn't care.

    if fred or jan or i wanted a homemade cake late
    at night, my mother would mix us up a little one.
    she seemed to understand that the world on the
        outside
    wasn't so easy for us...
        and she put all the love
            she could put into our hours at home.
        you should see the little cradles she made me out
            of oatmeal boxes.

    in hawaii the church owned a big old jeep we called
    the "carryall." it was UGLY. every morning my dad
    would take us to school in it. we would crawl down
    under the dashboard so no one would see us. we were
    horrified at the thought of ANYONE knowing
        that it was ours.
            they wouldn't like us as well.
                children can be cruel....

    about a block from school, my dad would stop.
        we'd open the door of the carryall a
            crack and make sure no one was around.
    we'd jump out and walk the rest of the way.
    i dreamed of what it would be like to pull up in front
        of the school in a fancy car like some other kids did.

    two Christmases we couldn't afford a Christmas tree.
    my mother never complained.
    she would ease our tears by making us think

some bamboo branches, sprayed gold, would be
       exotic.

    she would find out, through the newspapers, which
       churches
    were giving big Christmas programs, and we'd all
       dress up and go. she taught us to
          appreciate color and production and
             grand displays of pomp and ceremony.

    come to think about it, i NEVER remember my
    mother being unhappy about our financial status or
    the things she had to do without...
       our not having things 'most everyone else had.
          i don't recall her EVER complaining about
             where
    God had called my father or anything that call
    involved. without any conversation on it, she instilled
    in us the ability to be happy anywhere...
       that a lot of life doesn't go on down in our hearts
          where we FEEL...
             but in our HEADS where we DECIDE to be
             happy or
             unhappy.

    my father is a pray-er.
    when my brother was three, someone asked him what
    his father did, and he thought a minute and said,
    "he prays..."
    smile.
    over and over, mother told us growing up,
       "we'll all make it to heaven
          because of daddy ... daddy's prayers will
             bring us all through...."

24   i can never remember going to sleep at night
        but that my father was either walking the
        living room
            or pacing the patio outside
                praying.
        it was always safe to go check on my mom.
        if she was asleep, i knew everything would be all right.
            whatever my father was forcefully praying about
                wasn't too serious, or my mother wouldn't be
                    sleeping.

        what a wonderful combination!
        a father who has prayed me through all the
            years of my life ... and a mother who is
        just as much a Christian, but has kept me balanced
        between the ethereal and the practical.

        to us children, my father would say,
        "you can dream any dream ... and if Jesus
            lives in your dreams, and you are willing to
                work hard enough, and wait long enough,
            your dreams will live."

        my parents never protected me from pain. i
        remember them both crying with me through some
        rough times, but they continually reminded me that
        pain is a part of life...
        a part of God's plan of growth in me.
        it must have taken courage for them, but they
            kept pushing us out to face life on our own,
                promising us their love and God's faithfulness.

        today, when people say,
        "oh, ann, we so hope you stay the way you are...

and the world around you doesn't harden or
             change you,"

i respond,
"my parents are praying for me.
    they taught me from the crib, nearly, that
        there is only one thing that really matters...
    that's JESUS...
it's a foundation in my life ... it will follow me
    wherever i go."

a friend of mine is a wonderful example of a father.
from the time his children were born, his wife says
that he never left for work without going in and
kissing them goodbye...
    sound asleep. she says for all these years (they
    are now grown) he still goes in and kisses them
    when they are home. they had love
bestowed on them before they ever awakened every
day of their growing-up years.

    one day, i heard this man pray,
        "Jesus, make me the kind of father you
            need me to be...."

when children hear their parents pray,
it makes a difference. there is something about
an honest prayer from fathers and mothers that
makes a child want to be
something better.

one of this man's sons is about 6'6''. they were in a big
airport, and the father was getting ready to board the
plane for a business trip. there, in front of all those

people, his son leaned down and hugged and kissed
his dad.
    history stopped for one brief
    second, and the world understood
      love.
God's promise was:
honor your father and mother
    that your days may be long upon the land...
my father and mother have made ALL the difference
in my life. so often, people ask me why i love God so
much and why i seem to feel so assured of His love. it
dawned on me that if i have ever thought of God
being like my father,
    then all my life i've grown up
    loving and feeling loved by Him.
my father brought God, in His greatest
and purest beauty, to me...
and my mother reaffirmed it by allowing Him
    to create the atmosphere of our home.

my parents have never been written up in any big
article...
    or been talked about in a book other than mine...
      or been hosted by famous people.
      my father has never preached in great crusades.
they have just lived pure, strong, faithful, godly
lives ... fought good battles...
    kept the faith...
      established Jesus as Lord...
and raised me and my sister and brother.
the three of us think they are VIPs.

every time i stand in front of several thousand people
    to speak, i think of my dad. probably, deep down

27 inside, he's dreamed of a moment like that. as a
preacher, his crowds were always much smaller. i
think of my dad as i stand there, and i know
in a special way
  i not only represent Jesus...
i represent my dad and mom, too.
because they laid my foundation. they
are a part of every human being Jesus and i
touch.

they are moving the world, too.

confession

29   it's incredible, but
sharing all my victories has never made me secure.
some days, i had several good victories,
and sometimes, i had none ... but it didn't make any
difference. through it all, i was very insecure.

five years ago, when i became dean of women at
eastern nazarene college, not only was i one of the
youngest deans in america, but my predecessor was
MUCH older than i. hardly ANYONE really
liked me. for the first time in my life, i became
honest. there was no other choice.

five years ago, i couldn't have told you many things
that today i feel are important for you to know
about me. it matters that you know the WHOLE me.
before, i would have wanted you to
think i was wonderful, and today, i know i have
nothing to offer you and Jesus unless i am REAL.

there is something about confession that is so painful,
but totally healing.

i'd like to confess some things to you that you might
not guess about me.

sometimes, i feel threatened.
a student came to our campus, and she was full of life
and color, and she LOVED ME. when you are dean of
women, not everyone loves you,
and i loved being loved.

she'd bring me roses or a pepsi, or stick her head in
and smile. then ... about a year ago ...

30   i hired a sharp young couple to live in the
       women's dorm. the husband is an English professor,
       and the wife a drama teacher.
       she is beautiful inside and out.
       i began to notice that this student
       hardly ever again stopped by my office.
       if she did, she always talked about how neat "ronda"
       was.
       i thought she was, too, and i wanted the girls to feel
       that way about her, but one day i said to myself,

           "ann, you aren't jealous, are you?
              ann, i think you are..."

       imagine!
       i called the student in.
           "dawn, you are a student, and i am the dean ...
           but i want to tell you something. i think i feel
           threatened by yours and ronda's friendship. you
           keep talking about her and how beautiful she is,
           and i think she is, too ... but i don't feel very
           special
              any more...."

       my student looked at me.
       she seemed to say ... "ann, there has to be room in my
          life for lots
          of people..."
       and, of course, there must be room in MY life, too,
          because i meet new people every day.

       in that moment of honesty, i was healed. i loved
       ronda, and i loved dawn, and they loved me and each
       other. what really mattered to Jesus wasn't that i felt

jealous. He allows me the freedom to be a human
being, and that is a recognizable, human emotion ...
Jesus DID care that i be honest
    about it, and confess it, and face it ... and allow Him
        to teach me through it.

there are walls between people for all kinds of
reasons. i think it's mainly because so many Christians
are superficial. they refuse to confess their
deep-down, human struggles. they build barriers
instead.

last december, i was home with my family. it was SO
    SPECIAL.
    but i had accepted a convention in atlanta for
    new year's eve, and i had to say "goodbye,"
    knowing i'd spend another new year's eve alone.

we got to the airport late.
the gate area was packed.

"sir ... i'd like an aisle seat as close to the
    front as possible."

he slapped "19C" on my ticket and told me to get on.
i was late.

"19C ... sir ... PLEASE ... i don't like sitting in the back
seat of the plane ... i get sick ... it doesn't agree with
me...."

he looked up coolly, and said,
"lady, take it or leave it ... it's the
    last seat available. i told you ... you're LATE."

32   i grabbed my ticket and threw a stony look at him.
"oh, delta airlines, you make me TIRED!"

and i travel to talk about God's love.

as i started to tell my family goodbye, i stopped, and
said, "i must apologize..."

my sister said, "the agent is right behind you."

i turned around and broke into tears.
"sir, will you forgive me? i didn't mean to act like that.
    i don't usually. you see, sir, it's hard leaving my
        family,
        and i fly every week ... and i'm SORRY...."

the look on his face.
he didn't know what to do.

"lady, don't cry ... you weren't THAT terrible..."

finding my seat on the plane, i fell in, still crying,
and said ... "o Jesus, thank you for showing me what i
    really
    am when i am not in touch with you, thank you for
        loving me
        even when i embarrass you. Jesus, make me what
            you want me
            to be...."

                only Jesus can smooth the rough edges of
                    my life.
                He is my only hope in refining the
                    humanity called ann.

33   something else i've struggled with is my tendency to exaggerate. years ago, when a friend called this to my attention, i was DEFENSIVE. how dare she make a judgment like that. i've learned now to say "thank you," and to see that there is at least a tinge of truth in EVERYTHING critical.

in my book *i'm out to change my world* i told about my amazing youth group that grew from 88 to 400. oh, there were days when we had 400 from sunday to sunday, and sometimes a few more than 100, but i want to confess to you that never did we, over an EXTENDED period of time, have such a large group. you can see how insecure i was.
    Just coloring the truth a little made it look as if
        i was more effective than i really was ... and i
            ask you to forgive me.

even now, i retrace my stories. i ask people if i have told them accurately. often, i check with my secretary, gayla, to make sure i'm not "talking big."
    that kind of honesty really hurts.
        not just a surface hurt. it digs right down to
          the gut-level of our lives.
            but Jesus knew the secret ... OBEDIENCE.
            i not only want to hear what He is saying
            to me
            about ME, i want to obey...
    "YES, LORD...."

maybe you are different, but i just cannot completely change overnight. over and over, i give myself a stiff, critical review. i so desire to be what you and Jesus need me to be.

34   as i surrender each part of my life to God every day, i
       feel His spirit bearing witness with mine...
       and i'm growing. you'll see!

       oh, there are other things, too.
       my fear of failure...
          of having no one like my writing
          or having people like my writing and my speaking,
             but not really loving me as a person separate
                from that.
       there is loneliness as i fly thousands of miles
       every week. sometimes, when i stumble through an
          airport corridor to change planes, i cry. i don't care
             WHO sees me. i keep whispering,
                "o Jesus, i'm so glad You're my Friend.
                   i NEED You."
       BUT
       God made me as i am.
       He willed my being.
       i try to thank Him not only for the parts of me
          that please Him, but also for the flaws, knowing
             those level my life, and make me more
                compassionate toward your struggles.

       my sister, jan, who is a professional psychologist,
       comes to see me when her husband is out of town on
       business, and we have little "therapy" sessions.

       "ann, i've been thinking. do you have to talk so much
          when you're in a group? you have a tendency just
             to dominate
             the conversation...."

       "you know, jan, you're right, i do. i must work on that.

i keep thinking everyone wants to hear all my
        experiences."

we laugh, but i know i need growth in that area...
even today, i confess to you that STILL i have a
   tendency
to take over a group's interaction. sighhhh.

it's INCREDIBLE that i can sit here and confess all
   this
to you, and feel WONDERFUL. now you know.
      you can accept or reject me, but you KNOW.
         i have nothing to hide.
         i can live free.

c. s. lewis says that for whatever capacity there is in us
to be good, there is that same capacity in us for bad.

whoever around me has gone to prison,
      or been bankrupt, or fallen from the
         good graces of their fellowmen, or failed
            in a relationship...
"there go i but for the grace of God."

"in my hands no price i bring...
      simply to the Cross i cling."

alleluia.

no one is unimportant

37   i wonder how many church
officials ever take the janitor out
after church for steak and dessert.

   i wonder how much time the president of a
company spends with the people at the bottom
of the ladder...
just listening to their ideas...
sharing a cup of coffee and learning,
now and then, from someone other than
the corporate vice-president in charge of
promotion.

how many times, if i were given the choice, would i
spend an evening with a quiet, timid, totally unknown
person rather than a prominent, articulate,
stimulating, famous one?

i was just wondering.

i know a man who married young,
and after two children, while he was still in college,
his wife deserted them.
now, ten or eleven years later, he is raising the
children alone.

   they all three clean house together...
and cook and take turns doing the laundry.
they depend on each other.

the father hasn't been able to finish college. his
dreams of being a great preacher have faded. he has
spent all his energy in loving his children, and
working hard to keep them fed and happy, and being

both
father and mother.

recently, a friend of this man came to church to do a
Christian concert. the friend finished college and
looks pretty suave, and has had some good breaks.
now, he sings before large audiences about the "love
of God." but when bill walked up to him, an old
buddy, and tried to resume a friendship, the "great
artist" had no time for him. he was on to bigger and
better things than a part-time mother for a friend.
sigh.

anyway,
i think the father of two children, such as this one,
would win in character rating and true heart.
hardship and struggle tend to do positive things
like that in us.

Jesus says,
the first shall be last ... and the last, first...
He also says
the poor in spirit shall inherit the earth...
it's incredible,
but i think most of us are very aware
of everyone else's "position" or status in life.

as a little girl, i remember the evangelical world being
very interested in how big a minister's church was...
    how "influential" the members.
i know some ministers who almost feel they must tell
    lies in
yearly reports in order to keep up with the pressure
    of

39   reaching certain goals. they had
      better make so many calls, and win so many souls,
          and get so many to join the church, and
              sell so many church magazines, or
      they are in TROUBLE.

      some people pick a church to attend because
      people are more educated there or drive nicer cars
      or seem to have more money.

      in my church, if you were once a pastor, and then
      were promoted to an administrative position
      somewhere, you REALLY counted. as a little girl i
      remember knowing exactly who the "district
      superintendent" was ... and the college trustees. i
      learned to build a part of my worth around how many
      of these people knew me by name and acknowledged
      me.

      today, when i am insecure in a group,
      i find myself "name dropping" ...
      making sure the people around me know
      that some "more important" folks are my friends.

      i heard jill briscoe say,
      "NO ONE is unimportant..."

      often, though, i hear people talk ... and ME talk...

          "i went jogging with a LAWYER friend...'
          "i visited david ... DR. david rhodes..."
          "he's head of a LARGE hospital..."
          "this is paul ... his father is a PROMINENT
              doctor..."

40   our dear God,
forgive us.

what insecurity is there in the foundation of our
lives to make us so competitive to prove our worth?

a man who pours his heart out in some small,
    deserted spot...
who never builds the "greatest urban church" ...
must have enormous courage and stout heart.

all the people in the world
who have poured their BEST into every day,
and given years of earnest service in Christ's Name,
must be very cherished by Him.
He always judges our hearts
more than the visible results.
the church janitors and streetsweepers and
    bricklayers
and gas station attendants and factory workers ... well,
who ever decided that THEY
aren't the great people of the world?
    that THEIR ideas don't have the
        greatest weight?

if Jesus told all the "great Christians" of the world
that on a certain day He would be watching closely,
making His final judgment on us, i think
i know what we would all try to do...
we'd suddenly be scurrying around to "the least of
    these"
in our neighborhoods,
    on our jobs,
        at our schools.

41   probably, we would try to remember all the people
     we'd overlooked before. suddenly, i would notice all
     the simple, unexpected gestures around me.

     we'd be fervently loving the dirty and obnoxious and
        illiterate and immoral and troublesome souls
           next door and across the street and at the corner
           store.

     for one day, maybe real truth would live in our lives.
     maybe we wouldn't waste time and energy
     on all the nonessentials.

     i don't know...
     just maybe.

gardens

43   you would love this little lady.
ninety-seven years old!
when i met her, she was "out back" lifting
   heavy rock, trying to landscape one little
   piece of her yard that she thought looked
   imperfect.

i noticed her hands.
creased and worn, but perfectly
steady. she never used glasses to read
ANYTHING. her hearing was perfect.
well-dressed and groomed, she lived alone,
and did all her own housecleaning.

at ninety-seven, she is still painting large canvases
with bright, vivid colors
   and selling them.
     she makes beautiful rugs,
designed by herself. a marvelous garden flourishes
in the back yard. a couple of years ago, only because
of her age, they took her driver's license away.

"eloise...
   you've been a performer—pianist and singer.
     you're an established artist ... and have traveled
       abroad.
   out of all your experiences in life, what has given
     you the greatest satisfaction?"

"my garden..."

colors and perfumed petals and little buds sprouting
   and fresh tomatoes and small, red beets and
     spring onions....

"what do you dislike?"

"DISLIKE?" her face in a deep frown and her voice
    snapping.

"well, you know ... washing dishes or ironing or
    scrubbing or cleaning up your yard..."

"whatever there is to be done, I LIKE IT!"

her two favorite things are wood and manure.

"things grow so well in manure ... and just about
    anything wonderful can be created with wood..."

what an extraordinary human being.
she believes she was born to be creative with every day
in her life ... that God believes in hard work,
    and a positive spirit. there should be much wonder
        and joy over watching things grow,
            in the out-of-doors.

faithfulness to create the MOST with all the talents
    He
has given brings responsibility and a sense of
    well-being...
        even when it's down-home,
            hard work.

often, i've read the story in the new testament
about Jesus and the talents. suddenly, i think i
understand exactly what He meant. He will judge us
not by how good someone else is,
        or by how spectacularly we measure out one day.

45   He will watch our lifelong endeavor to take
          EVERY day and every hour and put whatever
             our best is into
       it. maybe no one around will pat us on the back,
       or praise us, but HE KNOWS.

       a friend of mine was approaching the intersection of
       a busy street. he was braking, because he could see
          someone
       ahead, crossing. as he got close,
       he noticed a small boy with his dog.
          the boy put himself and his bicycle between the dog
          and the car. he dared the car to hit him before it
             would dare touch his dog. as he crossed with the
             little dog, he glared at the car fiercely.

       for one moment, one small boy touched history with a
       profound gesture of love. it was his best.

       artur rubinstein, the concert pianist,
       was admired by many. a journalist approached him
       one day at the piano...

          "mr. rubinstein, i would give ANYTHING
             if i could play the piano like that..."

       to
       which
       rubinstein replied:

          "no, you wouldn't! i have bowed my knee to
          the goddess of the piano four hours a day for
             sixty-five years...."

46 was it edison who said that "genius is 2 percent
        inspiration,
    and 98 percent perspiration"?

    this week i addressed a group outside pittsburgh.
    a lady asked if i would stay with her family. there
    were many homes far more beautiful than hers, she
        said,
    and i could stay in a motel...
        but she let me know how much she and her
            husband would love to have me in the home
                that was THEIR world.

    i stayed in that little house.
    in the master bedroom.
    simple and small, but i could tell that the sheets and
        blankets were brand-new. the towels in the
            bathroom were new. as i sat at the kitchen
            table the next morning, there was an envelope
            with my name on it.
    blanche, this quiet, middle-aged woman, got up at
        five a.m.
    unable to sleep with excitement, and wrote...

        "ann, your coming to stay with us is as if Jesus
        had come. we are ordinary people. we don't have
        education or material possessions, but Jesus
        must love ordinary people because there are so
        many of us...
            and He sent us you."

    they gave their very best.
    i will never be the same.

47 many people come to boston, and call, and visit me. i remember one family especially because they had never been able to afford a real vacation until this summer. they put together a four-day yard sale where they live in memphis, and each member of the family contributed some prized possessions. they chose to come as far north as boston, and called, saying they had read my books and wondered if they could stop by. they insisted on buying my dinner, and i could tell it was a sacrificial chunk out of their vacation money.

they loved me and they dreamed, too.
they came clear from memphis to tell me.
it took a lot of TALENT to put that
trip together. it took wholehearted
effort. most of us barely scratch the potential
of our talents, and God never has enough to
grab on to and bless, really bless.

michelle is six. she ran up to me in a stadium after i had spoken. she handed me a little chain necklace, and asked if i would wear it. immediately, i put it on, and knelt by her so i could hug her. she looked at me, and said,

"you know what, ann?"
"what?"
"i'm a dreamer, too..."

some of my favorite people are percy and marie. at the age of eleven, percy was a baker. he would be at work at four a.m., and had to walk two miles in the country to get there.

at eighteen, he was baking for 450 men, and at
twenty, he was the town baker, making 350
loaves of bread, alone, every day.

his wife, marie, would drive over to the government
project every day, and go door-to-door to see how
people were. whatever they needed, she got it for
them...
    sweaters and coats and school dresses
        and groceries
            and a lot of love.
she had to keep a bottle of antiseptic in the car to wash
with afterward because there was so much filth.

every sunday, percy and marie would fill their car and
an old panel truck with children for sunday school.
    then they got a bus because
        they often picked up ninety at one time.
one lady had three-month-old twins. they would drive
out ten miles every sunday to get her ... and today,
those babies are twenty-six years old, and the goldins
still pick up their mother for church.

one night around midnight, the phone rang,
and percy answered. shortly, he was up, pulling on
his clothes and getting ready to leave the house.

    "some man called, and he needs a check
    to help him get his car fixed, and it's pouring
    rain, and i figured i oughta go see what i
    can do ... his name is john."

    "john who?" marie asked.

"i don't know ... just john."

this couple didn't find Jesus until they were
middle-aged. today they are in their seventies, but
you'd never know it.
   healthy.
      full of vitality and enthusiasm.
         still baking me biscuits when i stop
in houston ... and still making me go to their sunday
school if i'm there overnight on a saturday. i don't
know of ANY people who have done more with their
talents than percy and marie, and it shows in their
eyes,
      their strong handshake,
         their free laughter.

oh, i wish for hours and hours of gentle spirits and
easy laughter. clear eyes and warm handshakes.
   forgiving hearts and unselfish pocketbooks.

hours and hours of little touches of brilliance
   in everyday history.
      mary and her perfume.
         paul and a song in jail.
            Jesus spending the afternoon with
               zacchaeus
   or washing the tired feet of His followers
   or simply holding a child
      on His lap.

i want to grow a garden in my little piece of the world.
i want to plant ann's BEST into every day, and
SOME day, our Lord can say...
   "well done, thou good and FAITHFUL servant."

jennie

last week, my friend victor oliver flew in.
he is the editor-in-chief of tyndale, and we were going
to talk about this book.

i thought we should have lunch across the street at
this very nice restaurant because that is a piece of MY
world. it is my neighborhood. i know the manager,
and hostesses,
   and some of the waitresses. i want to love them
   to Jesus. we were seated in a section that was rather
      quiet,
      and i didn't know jennie, the waitress serving us.

"jennie, is karen working today?"
"no ... her day off..."
"please tell her ann said hello..."
"i know who you are ... you're the lady who writes
   books."

"i AM..." i was delighted!

"ann, are you a born-again Christian?"

"i AM ... are you?"

"no..."

"jennie, would you like to run over to my apartment
after work and talk to me?"

she said she would.
and she came.
we talked and talked and drank hot tea.
she cried. i cried.

she sang me a song she had once learned,
and i sang her one.

right there in my living room,
on an everyday monday night,
i told jennie that Jesus lived for her and IT DIDN'T
   MATTER
what she had done. Jesus was love.

"could we kneel, ann?"

there, side by side, we knelt, and jennie said,
"i'll pray."

never had i heard such a simple, pure confession.

"oh, Jesus, i am a terrible sinner, but ann says you
   forgive ANYONE.
   i am jealous.
   i am an adulteress.
   i lie and steal and am a poor wife and a
      bad mother.
   ann still says you love me and will accept me.
   forgive me, dear Jesus, and live in my heart."

we cried together, and Jesus came to us.
He always does.
there are so many people in the world who aren't as
honest as jennie ... that bare. so many who would be
   ashamed to confess all those secret spots.
but then, there's jennie.
God bless.
God bless.

she said she had many friends who didn't have much.
i figured maybe she didn't either.
finding a big cart on wheels down the hall, i began
to load it with sheets and towels and dresses and shirts
and nightgowns and coats from my closet. i gave her a
gaither trio record.

together, we pushed the cart into the elevator
and out onto the sidewalk and down the street to her
    car.

jennie, with black eyes swimming with tears, said,
"oh, ann, i feel like a little girl again.
i'm brand new inside. i have Jesus. thank you, ann,
for being my friend..."

i threw my arms around her.
it's incredible that an ordinary week night
can bring such beauty. i never knew jennie before,
and suddenly dreams lived,
and Jesus did ... in a new way ... He took
    jennie right where she was...
and love covered the night.

one more Christian to walk side-by-side with me
in my neighborhood.
yahooooo.

i ran back to my apartment crying.
the challenge of my life is trying to be what Jesus
    would
be if He lived in person where i do.

a religion editor of a large city paper interviewed me,

54   and he repeatedly asked,
      "what is an ambition of yours?"

      "to be a real Christian where i live...."

      "no ... no ... i don't mean that ... don't you ever want to
         write for a certain paper and sell a certain number
         of books or go to a particular foreign country or
         receive a special award?"

      "no, sir ... i really don't ... the single desire of my life is
         to follow Jesus..."

      following Jesus
      means finding jennies in my world.
      and the jennies make ALL THE DIFFERENCE.

alicia

55 i am going to tell you a story
that shows how very little i know about
God's love.

after addressing a group at west point,
i had one day to spend in boston before
flying on to anchorage, alaska.
my phone rang early in the morning.

"ann, this is alicia..."
"alicia?"
"yes, you know ... i called you a long time ago ... i live
    in iowa."

"oh, you read one of my books, didn't you..."
and i burst into smiles.

"ann, i've saved all my money and have run away
    from home.
i've come to move in with you."

"ALICIA! oh, alicia ... you can't do that. i just have
    one bed,
and i fly out early in the morning, and ..."
she burst into tears. she and her mother didn't get
    along.
someone had already stolen her suitcase with her
    purse locked in it.
she had no clothes.

i was ready to give her my whole wardrobe ...
    ANYTHING ... i just
didn't want to give her ME.

"alicia, what size do you wear?"
        "20"

i wear a 6 or an 8, and could see i wasn't going to
get out of this dilemma very smoothly.
"oh, Jesus ... HELP! what do You want me to do?"

after an hour on the phone, where i listened and
        counseled,
we both decided i would leave $50 cash in the lobby of
        my building,
and she would pick it up and take the next bus back to
        iowa.
        one should never run away from the problem.
        alicia should stay home and face the situation, and
        allow God room to help and heal.

after lunch with a lady in boston, i had an afternoon
of work scheduled, and a dinner appointment with
one of my neighbors. as i was hurrying
        into the lobby where i live, i noticed a girl
        sitting on one of the benches...
        it HAD to be alicia.
it was raining outside, and her hair was soaked with
little curls clinging around her face. she was hunched
over, and pathetic. she followed me to the elevator
and up to my apartment.
i was miserable.
it's so easy to love people who look good
and smell good and act good...
ACT GOOD ... alicia was going to move in with me....

we talked and talked.
for hours.

57   i fixed her stew and hot tea.
       nothing helped.
       finally, i suggested we pray.
       mainly, *i* needed it.

       "oh, Jesus, help me to be patient and to understand
       and to love alicia ... and help alicia to assume
       responsibility for her problems at home."

       and ... i added under my breath....

       "Jesus, you say if we've done it unto one of the least,
          we've
       done it unto You ... do you want me to put alicia in
          bed with me?
       I DON'T WANT HER MOVING IN!"

       well, i finally arranged for a "united way" worker to
       meet alicia the next morning and counsel with her
       after i flew out at 7 a.m. that night after four hours of
       praying, God suddenly and genuinely filled my heart
       with love for this sad girl. i crawled across the floor,
       and wrapped my arms around her, and cried with
       her.

       she was so lonely and so scared
       and so lost...

       i flew on to anchorage the next morning, and when i
       returned four days later, i checked with "united way."
       alicia had never showed.

          one thing i know.
          it is Jesus' love, and not ann's,

that will win.
ann fails.
she would have rather given
ANYTHING but herself.

"Jesus, walk with me. i need to learn a lot more about
love."

it's the "alicias" in the world that prove whether Jesus
is my Lord,
whether love is the vital force in my life.

everyday people on ordinary days

59   today, my friend had brunch with the queen.
he really did.

not everybody got invited.
that would be impossible.
i was one of many everyday people who didn't.

now, i'm getting ready to go to bed ... but
i wanted you to know i may be an everyday person,
but i had a great day.

i climbed on my ten-speed, and rode through
boston and along the charles river
with the wind in my face
and sun on my neck
and laughter.

later, i bathed and donned a long dress
and tied a ribbon around my head
and felt pretty.
jumping into a cab, i rode to a downtown
church, and walked in as if i belonged,
and felt the Presence of God.

tonight, there was a huge fireworks display
in the harbor, and i stood with thousands
of people, cheering and applauding.
the sky exploded with color and design, and
i felt GLAD...
glad to be alive.

you see, it's incredible, but everyone must create
his or her own color in each day.
it's not who we know

60   or what special events are chalked into our calendars.
      it's our WILL to be happy.
         to keep humor in the casualties.
            to commit an ordinary day to Jesus, and initiate
               our own adventure with HIS help.
      i dare you TODAY to find the mystery and surprise
      in this hour's simple piece of history. you'll see.

      in Christ, there is no queen or pauper.
      there IS potential for strong, great hearts
         and deep, moving love ... and
            people with destiny.
               destiny to turn war to peace
      and dissension to unity
      and indifference to love
      and a world made whole.

      my important friend,
      who shared the day with the queen, called
      and we tried to decide which one had the best day...
      he or i.

      guess what?
      it was unanimous...
      my day won.
      maybe because bikes and sunshine
      and total freedom to create are more exciting than
      being locked into the ceremony of a queen's visit...
      and tight shirt collar
      and frayed nerves about
      proper etiquette.

      if you WANT to,
      you can be happy wherever you are.

61   but then,
       it all depends on how hard
       you are willing to work at it.

       just remember...
       you have no idea what fun lies in
       one unknown, unscheduled day.
       allow Jesus to be your
       creative initiator.

anxiety

63   there is a story you would like.
      i read it in one of the popular magazines.
      it was about a lady who took her small children to the
         park.
      she was weary and discouraged.
         after putting her little son in a swing, and the
         baby in the grass, she plopped down on a park
         bench. a little bare-chested boy wearing only
         dirty cutoffs came up and said,

      "hiya, lady ... is that your baby?"

      "yes-s."

      "boy, you sure are a lucky lady, you got a baby... my
      mom said some day i might have a baby again. my
      baby died. you got a daddy, lady?"

      "yes, but he's in the hospital sick...."

      "wow, you're sure a lucky lady. you got a daddy and
      EVERYTHING. my momma said i once had a daddy,
      too ... but he wasn't a family man ... but she said i
      might have a daddy again sometime..."

      this small boy picked up a piece of string from the
      ground. it had many tiny knots in it, and he crawled
      up next to the young mother and let his legs swing.
      patiently, he began trying to unravel all the tight
      knots. after quite awhile, the lady gathered her
      children and told the little boy she'd have to be going.
      he smiled and said,

      "here ya are, lady ... it's a present."

and he handed her the string with all the knots undone, and the string straightened. she thanked him, tucked it in her pocket, and headed home. her little boy noticed she was SMILING, and was rather amazed.

"mom, how come you're happy now. you sure weren't when we came to the park..."

she let loose of his hand and dug into her skirt pocket and felt the smooth piece of string. she thought of how that was like God. He takes the rough parts of our lives, and, if we give Him time, He unties the knots and straightens the kinks...

"oh," she said, "i'm such a lucky lady. i have a daddy and everything..."

that lady went to the park discouraged,
unhappy, worried, she forgot there were any
positives ... there was not one touch
   of yellow
    in her sky of gray.
     she forgot to look.
i wonder if ANYONE has had a day like mine. my car is parked downstairs with four flower pots on their sides on the floor ... with dirt spilled and piled everywhere. the earnest young plants are without soil to dig their roots in. they all toppled on my way home from work at eleven p.m.

after a fifteen-hour day.

every time my phone rang today, i was hoping it

would be some surprise call with extraordinary
promise for my tomorrows ...
but every call was from
> the housekeeper in one of the dorms
> or a girl without a room for next year
> or a speaking invitation i had to say "no" to
> or a professor wanting to reserve a guest room
> or a lady who couldn't find my books in ANY
> bookstore.

my desk is still covered with unanswered mail and
> memos...
so many reminders of undone errands.

tonight, after a hot bath, i fell on my knees by
the open window and confessed my sin of intense
> anxiety and
worry.
> my forehead had a crease in it all day.
> my manners were terrible! i addressed envelopes
> > while people came in to speak to me.
> > > sighhhhh.

God doesn't make me tired and sick.
i do.
God doesn't even get a chance to try to carry my
burdens. i assume total responsibility, and leave God
somewhere in the dust while i become desperately
unnerved with fears and cares.

it is almost midnight, and today is finished. i cannot
remove the wear and tear that my inner anxieties
have caused in my mind and body. i cannot undo the
wasted hours ... of MY effort.

today, i forgot all the good.
i filled several hours with awful worry.
i didn't feel the wind on my face or smell the flowers
or lean back in my chair and breathe deeply and think
great, simple, quiet thoughts.
i didn't feel glad to be alive, and hardly thought of
anyone but ME. even God barely squeaked an edge in
my thoughts. so much of today was wasted on the
   ridiculous,
nonessentials to my destiny.

c. s. lewis says our greatest strengths are also
our most vulnerable points of weakness. it's true.
it is good that i work hard...
   that i feel intensely about the pain and hurt
     of the world ... that i get up every morning and
      tear into life full-force and want to get A LOT
      accomplished.
but it is too bad
that i forget Jesus can accomplish
even MORE through my efforts if i am relaxed
and poised and yielded in His hands.

i am ashamed. too often i forget
that Jesus is far more interested in
   heart-to-heart chats
     and time to play catch with the child
     up the street and a cup of tea
     with a neighbor....

He cares that men be dads
and ministers learn how to laugh easily.
that we build relationships, and sit back and dream
   sometimes...

67   He wants us to "run and NOT BE WEARY..."
         to "walk and NOT FAINT..."
    He says WAIT on me
    and you can ride easy...
        swing with the punches...
            adapt and adjust without wrinkle lines and
                frayed emotions....

    "Jesus, today i've been anxious for EVERYTHING.
    this is sin.
    i confess it.
    take the intensity of my life
        and channel it into smooth-flowing gestures
        and uncomplicated, paced hours."

    amen. amen.
    tomorrow, God and i will try again.

miracles

i recently met a lady who had just
lost four of her six children in an
automobile accident.

she still came to the convention,
played the piano.
she cried, but she laughed, too.
    participated in the games...
        sang with her whole heart.

for her and her husband to accept this tragedy in
    their lives...
    to believe in God's ability to turn sorrow
        into "something beautiful"...
            for me, this is a true miracle.
            a miracle of healing.

six years ago, the greatest miracle of my life
was pat boone's coming to my youth group in
    california.
for the rest of my life, i will be indebted to God
    and to pat for that extraordinary gesture.

today, many people wish for a "pat boone" in their
worlds ... but i see miracles far greater all around us.

    my sister addressed a dinner, and afterward,
    a lovely couple came up to visit. jan asked,

    "do you have children?"
    "yes ... we have two. one is with the Lord, and one is
        thirteen."

they proceeded to tell jan that one of their children

70   was very healthy until he was three. suddenly, he developed a brain tumor, and in a matter of weeks, was gone.

they weren't bitter.
their child was still their child...
only now he lived with the Lord.
to have such a SPIRIT is miraculous!

our greatest growth...
EVERY miracle...
comes to us out of
adversity.

so many people today move from place to place. one friend of mine, a mother of three, had moved six times in the last few years with her husband's changes of jobs. her husband came in, announcing that another move was necessary.
she felt she couldn't pack and unpack again.
she just COULDN'T.

one day, under warm, clear sky, she put the children, along with a picnic lunch, in the car and headed for the beach.
there were thousands of people.
everyone absorbing the sun and water on a
hot, humid day.
this young mother sat and watched the ocean,
and lay back and tried to scan the wideness and
depth of blue in the sky.
usually that quieted the anxiety and
pounding in her heart ... but today,
it meant nothing.

she was tired.
she didn't want to face life.

suddenly, she missed michelle, her five-year-old.
jumping up, she noticed the lifeguard running out to
the water, and a few minutes later, he brought little
michelle, wet and coughing, to her mother.

if God could help that lifeguard pick
out that little girl on a huge beach with
    several thousand people ... if God could help
        him rescue her...
then Jesus could help this mother take the
challenge of another move...
    and come through with victory.
        she accepted the task.

oh, the miracle of allowing God to help us
    deal with the realities of life!

a woman found her husband having an affair.
she was faced with the decision of divorce
    or living with him.
        there was so much bitterness and hurt.

she said,
    "the miracle came when i was able to SURRENDER
    this to Jesus. i told my husband i was sorry for
    the hate and bitterness i had built into our home
    because of my hurt. i apologized to my
    children for my wrong spirit."

the miracle of one person finding new resources for
happiness ... of not allowing something that could be

devastating to destroy her inner peace and beauty.
she began rebuilding, with God's help ... to plant
seeds of love and friendship in many places
she hadn't thought of before.
even today, i wear a lovely mauve pink dress she
made, with a ribbon the same
color tied around my head.

to surrender that kind of hurt and rebuild
must be one of the greatest miracles of all.
generations are built on that power.
her children's destinies can be changed for the
good.
it is a miracle for eternity.

last spring, i flew to seattle to speak.
it had been a long flight, and a three-hour time
change.
i was tired.
when i got off the plane, a young couple called
my name, and said they had asked to pick me up.
paula, their tiny three-year-old, was with them, and
i noticed
she had braces on her legs. we took turns carrying
her through the airport.

when we got to the car, paula wanted to
sit in the back seat with me.
"ya know what?"
"what?"
"i'm going to get a baby brother...."
"a baby brother ... WOW...."

the young mother didn't look as if

she was about to produce a baby, and i wondered where the baby was coming from.

julie turned around from the front seat, and said, "ann, i'd better explain something to you. i gave birth to a little boy three weeks ago, but he died last night, and his funeral is tomorrow. paula doesn't understand."

i felt overwhelmed
with pain and sadness.

"oh, mike and julie, you shouldn't have come to pick me up. i didn't know it was such a hard day for you."

mike responded...

"ann, we wanted to help you change the world. you spoke at our college before we graduated, and we asked God to move the world through us, too...."

julie went on to tell me that the doctor had called around midnight. the baby had only five or six minutes
left to live. he wondered if he could take the baby off the respirator, and hold him while he died. the baby, he said, was the bravest, most stouthearted newborn he'd ever seen. a few minutes later, he called to say the baby was gone. weeping, the doctor wondered if he could come to the funeral.

julie looked at me...

"ann, do you think we
        could love that doctor to Jesus?"

    "you can, julie...."

mike and julie and little paula came to hear me speak.
the next day, i attended the funeral where the young
doctor sat next to young parents who had lost their
little son.
    i wept.

before i flew back to boston, i asked
mike and julie...
    "how do you really feel?"

mike looked at me and said, "ann, we want Jesus
to move the world through us. maybe if we hadn't lost
aaron michael, we wouldn't know how to hurt with
people. paula has cerebral palsy,
and our dream is for her to walk.
maybe we needed dreams in our home
to understand impossible dreams in others' lives.
    ann ... you and God can count on us to help change
        the world...."

i boarded a plane for home,
    and i'll never be the same again.

to love means to be vulnerable...
    to allow God to put in
        or take out of our lives
            whatever He knows will make us sensitive to
            His Spirit,
            and to a dying world.

75   i do think there are miracles of new cars and nice
         houses
            and surprise visits from extraordinary people.
         BUT the greatest miracles, for me,
         are the paralyzed people who can still laugh and
            shed warmth,
               and create ... those who lose loved ones
      and don't remain bitter and questioning the rest of
         their lives,
            but rather allow God to work it for good....

      a miracle is a shy, insecure person finding
            self-acceptance and a sense of well-being.
         it's ann learning to like ann.

      it's the miracle of living with imperfections.
         God healing us from WITHIN,
               rather than changing an outward
                  circumstance...
            an internal touch that helps us to make the most
               of where we are...
            of accepting the things we cannot change.

      only Jesus can author miracles.
            did you know EVERYONE can have miracles?
         it's incredible ... but Jesus does things
               like that.

God's grace

77   his name is jack wright.
a long time ago, he was a preacher...
   married, and father of two daughters.
but somewhere,
he got all twisted and angry and bitter,
and he lost out.
   on his family.
      his ministry.
      himself.
he earned his doctorate in sociology, went
through another marriage, and became a successful
criminologist ... and
   it so happened he had graduated many years
      before from northwest nazarene college,
         where i attended.

one day, he read an interview about me from the
   college,
after i had been there to do a spring convention.
he called, and in a gruff sharp voice, he asked,
   "who is ann kiemel ... and how come everyone
     loves you?"

   "i'm an everyday young woman ... and not
   everyone loves me ...
     some don't even like me!"

an agnostic, he didn't even know where a Christian
bookstore was, but he hunted one up in new orleans,
and drove across town to find my books.
   he began to read them at the stoplights
   on the way home. a tape came with one of the
     books, and he started to listen to it, and began
       to cry and cry.

right there, in his living room,
after years and years of deserting Jesus
Christ and His love,
jack wright came home.

he wrote me recently...

"as you know, i am a runner, and one of my favorite
places to run is the levee that protects LSU from
the mississippi river. last week i was running,
and decided to run three miles instead of the usual
two. my running buddy fell a few yards behind,
and i began to think of how lonesome i was ...
and i remembered a phrase 'are you running with
me, Jesus?'
i thought of your childlike faith, ann, and
the adventure you had with the california football
team,
so i prayed:

'Jesus, would you run with me?
are you really out there, Jesus? my lungs burn
and
my legs ache and it's easier to run when
someone is beside you. show me, Jesus, that you
are really with me, in my life,
by running with me down this mississippi
levee.
please...
so my faith will be strengthened and i'll know
you'll be with me in the other problems of
life.'

ann, i began to feel the presence of Jesus...

79   i began to stretch out my pace, and in my mind's
             eye, i could see Jesus' sandaled foot matching my
                 pace, stride for stride. i could sense his
       carpenter's body, strong and muscular,
             running with me ... and i could almost see his
             long hair blowing in the wind.

         i lengthened my pace, again.
             usually, at the end of three miles,
       my lungs burn so ... i am breathing heavily, and
           my legs ache and i have to push myself to finish.

         but
         my lungs felt clean and full of oxygen, and
             i ran and ran and ran
                 like a schoolboy dashing home from
                     school ... and Jesus was with me every step
                 of the way. i crossed the three-mile point...
         stopped, and looked back for my friend.

             he was 800 yards behind me.
         and i wept and wept...
                 that Jesus would run with me
                 there on that mississippi levee....

         God ran with one of his children to strengthen my
             faith. when my friend caught up, he said,
                 panting,
             'what got into you?' "

       it's incredible
       what Jesus does
       with reborn
       creatures...

it's incredible
how easily He forgives and rebuilds and
patiently waits.
oh, how He loves people like jack!

and people like marla...
once an unwed mother, now in her second marriage,
a minister's wife, remade, and
being used by God's Spirit in her little
piece of the world.

marla understands when people ask her about
forgiveness. she first married when she was seventeen
years old. it seemed so perfect, so right ... but while
she was pregnant with their first child, she discovered
that her husband was having affairs with other
women.

one day, before the baby was born, david was on a
new motorcycle when a car hit him ... and his leg had
to be amputated. he was bitter. when the baby came,
he threatened to kill her when she cried, and to kill
marla, too.

eventually, she had to take the baby and flee for
safety. she began to work in a restaurant within
walking distance of the apartment.
a policeman would come in to eat on his rounds,
and was friendly to her ... and they found themselves
strongly attracted to each other. even though he was
married and had two little daughters, the attraction
was too strong to resist.

marla, brokenhearted, moved away ... but wherever

she moved, larry the policeman found her....
she loved him, and before long, she was
pregnant with his baby. moving again, she found a
duplex that would be cheaper and offer more room,
and she decided to have the baby and not intrude on
larry's marriage.

the couple that shared the other side of the
duplex were out working on a fence, when marla
went out to get acquainted. in the course of the
conversation, the neighbors mentioned they had
to go get ready for their church softball game.

marla asked which church...
well, could she go with them on sunday?
this church-going couple was shocked.
here was a hungry neighbor who had to INITIATE
the invitation to church.

the people in that little church loved marla,
and nurtured her. they helped her learn that Jesus
would forgive her even though she couldn't forgive
herself.

she gave birth to a boy, and named him
after his father ... whom she loved but
had no idea where he was. marla still
hadn't finished high school. she went at night,
and worked hard. even so, she ended up
on welfare.
and then
out of nowhere
larry showed up again.
it had been fifteen months.

this frightened, burdened young woman was
lonely and vulnerable ... and her one sexual
    encounter in fifteen months
        put her back into pregnancy.

"oh, ann, i couldn't believe it. i wanted to die.
    i was now not only a disgrace to my family, but
        to God. i claimed to be a Christian, and i loved
    the Lord Jesus, but i could only seem to make
        messes.
        i wanted to run. i couldn't face my church family.
    i had two children now, and we could hardly
        survive."

she went to the bathroom, and started to take every
pill she could find....
suddenly it seemed that the whole room
        was filled with the presence of God.
    she began to think of the words to a song
        that she had recently learned in church...

    "amazing grace ... how sweet the sound...
        that saved a WRETCH like me ... i once was
        lost ... but now, i'm found...
    was blind, but now i see."

there, in that bathroom, Jesus came
to marla. there...
    amid her sin and failure...
        He loved her and forgave her
            again.
        she found enough love to start over.

a loving church still cared.

83   they forgave her, too.
         i don't know where that church was, but
            Jesus must have been proud. a lot
      of churches today, i'm afraid, would
            have lost faith in marla, and deserted her.

      this time, marla knew she must give her baby up.
      somewhere in the world today that baby girl
      is now growing up in a loving home...
            somewhere where marla will never see her again
               until heaven.
                  and there must be many who understand that
                     same lifelong pain, that somewhere your
                  flesh and blood lives and moves apart
                     from you.

      but today, marla is married to a man
      who loves marla in spite of her past.
         he trusts her and believes in her and forgives
            her just as Jesus has....
               God has given them several more children,
         and their home is Christ-centered.

      you see,
      it does seem incredible...
         but that is how deep and how high and
            how wide God's love is.

      scars remain...
         yes.
      we reap what we sow...
         yes.
      but sins are forgiven.

marla is WHOLE
a fresh, new life is hers.

there is one more person
you must know...
hugh gorman.

british.
grew up in ireland.
from a family of the poor working class.
at seventeen, he joined the british army,
and for the four and a half years he served,
he spent most of his time
     being punished for various offenses.
          drunk, absent without leave, insubordinate,
               disobeying orders, burglarizing, threatening
                    to kill.
much of his time was spent
in solitary confinement on
bread and water.

finally, after a dishonorable discharge, he was
released from prison, and told never to join her
majesty's forces again.

hugh had great ideas about how he was going to live,
but he started in on great drinking sprees. he
stole money, robbed stores and people.
     he terrorized ... and caused ugly scenes
          in the streets of belfast.

he says he first drank to enjoy the company of good
     friends ... then to forget the things
he had done...

to get away from the
          person he had become.

"ann, in my heart, i hated the person i was...
     i hated myself more than any other person in all
          the world. even as i tell you, i must cry...."

one saturday night, he came out of a bar
in ireland, and there
     at the corner
     was a street meeting.
the minister said, "gorman, God can change your
     life!"

hugh laughed at the man.
he didn't believe him.
nothing could change his life.
     his parents had tried and failed.
          the army had failed.
               the prison authorities couldn't. and
          even hugh gorman had tried to turn the course of
          his life ... and couldn't!

in his heart, as he walked away, he wished it were
     true.
if only he could start over again.
he didn't know that Jesus changed hearts.
he thought Christians just carried bibles under their
     arms.
that minister held street meetings faithfully.
over and over, he would meet gorman walking out of
     the bar.
"gorman ... God CAN change your life!"

86   one day, he invited hugh to a revival service.
he couldn't resist when the minister sent a young
girl with a bible to pick him up.

"the preacher talked about the love of Christ, ann...
    and said that Jesus loved even me. could it be
        true?"

he wanted someone to love him for himself.
many were afraid of him.
his father was ashamed of him.
parents were telling their children to "stay away
from hugh gorman ... he'll get you into trouble."
he wanted someone to love him,
and wondered if Jesus really did die
so his life could be changed.

they sang a hymn...

    "were the whole realm of nature mine,
    that were a present far too small.
    love so amazing, so divine,
    demands my soul, my life, my ALL...."

hugh says that before the appeal was made...
    before he raised his hand...
        before he went to the place of prayer...
    he had committed his life
to Christ.

what his parents tried so hard to do...
    and the british army had failed to do ... and what
        prison could never do in a million years,
Jesus Christ did in a moment.

87   today
hugh pastors a little church
in a small spot in canada.
his eyes sparkle and
   his spirit is radiant.
   with him and his wife, i have wept out
   my praise and thanksgiving.

the awesome power of the Holy Spirit tearing at our
   lives ... breaking us into a thousand pieces ...
   and as my friend bill jackson says...

"i lay before Him, completely naked...
   a sinner who needed grace.
   a warrior who needed new life:
     Holy Spirit energy that fleshes itself out
to kids and gas station attendants and ice cream men
   and waitresses...
a love that fears no evil,
   that laughs at the meager attempts of satan,
     that stands before a mountain and says,
   'in the Name and power of Jesus, move,'
   and the mountain crumbles,
   is leveled to the ground."

alleluia. alleluia. amen.

dependence

SOME PEOPLE don't know how to give love back.
they take and take...
   become dependent...
      and rather than growing from it,
      becoming strong by it,
they take advantage of others' time and effort.
they make everyone around them
responsible for their happiness.

i addressed a convention, and met a young girl who
had many problems. a group of women came to me
and said they had spent hours talking to her on the
phone...
   fed her many meals...
      gave her a bed in their homes...
and none of it seemed to help. they were frantic. after
one of the sessions, i noticed this girl was waiting to
talk to me.

      she told me no one loved her.
      the people in the church didn't care.
      her life was ruined
      ... and
      would i be her friend?
   i told her the reason she had no other friends
   was because she had drained them of all they
   had to offer. they had given and given, and had
   no energy left ... or resources ... to help her.

one day, after returning to boston, my
phone rang, and it was this girl.
   she was going to commit suicide.
   she had run away from home.
   she was sick of a world that didn't care.

i confess,
i was FURIOUS.
"a world that DOESN'T CARE?"
leslie had probably been shown more love
than most of us get in a lifetime.

    i refused to allow her to manipulate me into pity
    ... to reinforce her bad behavior, thinking a sob
    story to someone new would bring the attention
    she needed.
        i had accepted her collect, long-distance
        call, and i was happy to talk... but not about
        suicide. we needed to talk about some
        things SHE could do to allow God to help
        her over this rough spot.
many ministers and wives counsel people
long after midnight.
some people really want to change,
and use the time and love and advice as
    steppingstones.
some never do.
    it's just so easy to be unhappy,
        and dependent on someone else to make us
            feel good.
as a Christian, i struggle because i feel the
responsibility to care for people, but i know there is a
LIMIT to what i can give. i don't mind walking forty
extra miles with someone as long as i know they are
walking with me. that makes a difference!

i remember a student at the college.
she was insecure socially...
    had few friends...
        was really frightened in the world.

91   we spent hours together.
she wrote me journals of her feelings every day,
and we would try to plan ways
to make her feel more at ease with others,
more accepting of herself.
over and over, we prayed together.
my favorite scripture for this student was 1 peter 1:2:
    "may God bless you richly,
      and grant you increasing freedom
        from all anxiety and fear" (TLB).

marie began to live at my office. i think she watched
from her dorm window as i drove in every morning
because three minutes after i'd walk into my office,
she was there, too.

one day, i called her in.
this was going to be painful, i told her, and
she could cry because i'm sure i would, too.
i told her how very much i loved her and
believed in her...
    but i wasn't her whole world.
      i was just one person in that world, and there
        were many others out there...
    that it wasn't healthy for her to build all
her security around me. some day i would be gone,
    or she would graduate, and Jesus willed us to
      stretch the boundaries of our lives.

she must not spend so much time at my office.
she must find and develop other friendships.
i was insisting on this because i really loved her.

    she sobbed.

she was hurt.
i cried.
i understood.

it took several days for marie to recover,
but she did. she KNEW i loved her,
but not in a crippling kind of way.
we had little planning sessions on ways to improve her
    appearance,
and to get her involved with others.

today, she is a successful teacher.
she is one of the most marvelous people
i will ever know.
she accepted the challenge.
rather than just taking from me,
she began to plant seeds of friendship and love.
she did special things for people she worked for.
    she baked cookies and cakes for girls' birthdays on
        her dorm floor.
    she sewed girls' wedding dresses.
    her world GREW.

a lot of couples marry because
one or both are afraid of not surviving
without the other....
    their happiness is dependent
        on the other one's support and care.
        that isn't love.
        that is one person making another
        totally responsible for his or her
            well-being.

love can breathe and grow and live

93   when we not only receive it,
       but learn to give it back.

       it doesn't matter how much love we give to
       one other human being...
           unless that person is willing to start loving
               back ... to begin planting seeds of love
                   in his or her own back yard ...
               there can be no healing.

       it isn't healthy for us to allow people to
       demand
       that we be their sole supporters,
       their only source of love.
       we must draw boundaries.
           we must love ENOUGH to force them
               to assume responsibility for their own
                   happiness and well-being.
       if we let people manipulate us into thinking we
       must carry them on our backs for the rest of our lives,
       then we will never teach them that to walk,
           they must first take their own steps...
               and only God can lead them when they
                   are willing to do that.

       isn't it amazing and incredible!
       love IS only good
           "when you give it away...."

       "Jesus, teach us how to love others.
           make our love healthy. may we give all You
               desire us to give, and may we nurture just as You
                   would
                   if You were here in person...

94   but show us how to draw boundaries...
           and how to expect responsibility ... may strong
           people come from our love instead of weak
           and lame ones."

generosity

95   you reap what you sow.
you get back in life what you've
    put into it.
people treat you as you treat them.
one must earn the right to be heard.
    and GENEROSITY pays.

when students came into my office at
the college, and expressed great resentment and
hostility toward their parents, i always
reminded them,

      "if you treat your parents with respect
   and patience and understanding, some day your
     children will do that to you...."

one day, parents of one of the students came in to me.
   they were ANGRY!
   i had no expertise in my job, they said.
   i used poor judgment with their daughter...
     and they didn't just quietly tell me.
       sighhhh.

today, as i look back on it, i would probably
have made the same unpopular decision.
but it really doesn't matter
whether one of us was absolutely right
   or wrong.
   one thing was clear...
   either i was going to become defensive
     and bitter and brooding,
       or i was going to forgive them
     of the hurt i felt deep inside.

96   to be honest, my greatest inspiration in allowing
       Jesus to help me forgive was His warning:
          *i will forgive you in the same manner that
             you forgive others....*

       generosity affects every area of our lives,
          our attitudes and spirits,
             our natural ease and freedom.

       as a child, i remember my mother always feeding
       servicemen. meal after meal, whoever knocked on
       our door, she'd take them in...
          even one big, huge man from
          arkansas who ALWAYS ate more than his share.

       we'd cry.
       we didn't like always having to
       share our food with others.

       often my mother would remind us...
       "some day you children will be out in the
          world, and if i love and care for other mothers'
             children, God will bring people along to care
                for you."

       oh, my mom was right.
       fred and jan and i have reaped her love
       hundreds of times as people have loved and fed and
          housed us.

       some missionaries were returning from a foreign
       country. their daughter wasn't ready to face the
       abrupt changes that coming to america would bring.

again, my mother suggested that this girl stay with us
in hawaii
    "in the twins' bedroom"
      for several months.

   we didn't have my mother's heart.
   as little girls, we were selfish.
     our bedroom was already crowded with
     two of us in one small room.

but connie came.
we loved her.
the three of us made a team.
   i'm so glad we took connie in.
     there were lots of surprises ... and
       years later, the benners moved me into
         their guest room while i was teaching school
           and needed a place of love during hard
             times.

at Christmas, in our home,
we gave our best. often, opening our presents,
we would cry...
   with surprise.
     with spellbound hearts.
   each gift represented hard-earned money
     and much thought and ingenuity.
there was something special about that spirit.
putting our whole hearts into the gifts
made our enthusiasm explode.
God lived in BIG ways.

i've spoken in places where people gave me
just enough to get me home...

just enough so they could look me
           in the face when they handed me the envelope.

then...
there was that average-size church
that brought me in. after i had spoken
   and fallen in love with the people, it was
      time to leave. the pastor put an envelope in
   my hand, and said,
      "we all love you, ann...."

i thanked him, but didn't open the envelope.
never do i do that.
it's not an issue with me, so
i always wait until i get on the plane,
or arrive home.

after boarding the plane, i was going
through many little notes people had handed to me as
i was leaving, and suddenly i saw the envelope with
the check. i sat there stunned...
a huge amount!

i jumped up,
demanded they let me off the plane for just
a few minutes.
   running down the ramp, i began screaming,
   "rev. fletcher ... rev. fletcher ... i CANNOT take
      this ... it's TOO MUCH...."

   "it's yours, ann. it's what the people
      gave you...."

well, i cried all the way to chicago

where i changed planes.
no ... i didn't keep it all.
   after the tithe came out, there was so much left
   over to share ... a housekeeper on campus who
   needed a surprise ...
   a family man who needed a little boost.

those people who gave so freely
have no idea how many others
they touched because
they gave, so beautifully, in
Christ's Name.
it brought so many of us
such happiness.
those people are winners.
Jesus will repay!

He says, if you give to me, i will return...
   pressed down ... running over....

tom, my brother-in-law, is the financial
administrator of a hospital in cleveland.
he is thirty years old.
the pressures are great.
what i so admire about tom, though, is the fact
that he puts just as much effort and energy into his
church as he does his business...
   hours and hours of planning projects
   for the sunday school and the building program.
   he doesn't get paid at the church,
      but his priorities are right,
      his values...
   and SOMEDAY, it will be measured back to
him in the same manner in which he has given.

100   set a sack of groceries on someone's step.
        take time for a cup of tea with a neighbor.
          mow the elderly man's yard.
      whip up some warm cookies.
          stop and shake a hand.
            give a genuine smile.

      put a cool hand on a hot forehead...
        play five minutes of catch with the little boy
          up the block...
        share a lick of your ice cream cone...
          or a small bouquet of picked flowers.
      be one person who will listen.

        in whatever measure you give, you'll receive.
        this is God's principle.
        He promises.

    "o Jesus...
        help me to laugh freely and give without
          reservation...
        to make You the finance chairman of my money.

          may i reap the pleasure of watching many people
            find happiness because i've given all i could
              in Your Name...."

hair

101   one day a man called from a faraway city.
       he loved my books and tapes, but

       "i just want to know ... do you have a hair
           problem?"

       what an incredible question!

       "i beg your pardon...," sucking in my breath.

       "well, in all the pictures on your books, your
       hair is so short. i thought you must have a hair
       problem."

       "no ... i don't ... i just like short hair ... do you think
           EVERYONE who's read my books thinks the
               same thing?"

as badly as i wanted to be objective and level,
i cried and cried.
a hair problem!
well...
my head is one of my most vulnerable
places. i'm always struggling with my hair,
or thinking my bottom teeth are growing a little
crooked.

i began to pray.
"Jesus, i feel so insecure about my hair.
when i walk outside and smile at people,
i think they're smiling back not because they like me
but because they think i have a hair problem...
what should I do?"

now you may not think Jesus cares about my hair,
but i know He cares about how i feel about ME. after
a lot of prayer and private thought, i decided to let my
hair grow.

the next week, waiting for a cab in boston, a very
    refined,
handsome man was waiting beside me.

"young lady, i just LOVE your hair."

"You LOVE my hair? oh, please, sir ... don't love it.
thank you very much, but another man told me last
week that he thought i had a hair problem, so i just
decided to let it grow..."
sigh.
smile.

it hasn't been easy to let it grow.
i've pulled it back with barrettes and bobby pins,
and tied ribbons around my head,
and looked like a young squaw.

'most everyone likes it longer, but there are some
who wish it was still very short ... or that i'd
put a lot of permanent in it.

i give up.
you can never make everybody happy.
when my hair looks its worst,
and i've tried and tried, but there are
still some frizzies and wrong twists
of curl,
    and i still have to get up and

address a big audience of people,
            i realize they brought me
            not because of how i look, but because
            of what's in my heart.

            AND I MUST LAUGH.
            humor keeps the nerves easy
                and the tension low
                    and the beat of life even
                        and full of simple
            optimism.

            a couple of weeks ago, i was visiting
            jan, my sister. we both agreed HER hair
            needed a little improvement, and someone had
            recommended a particular beauty shop.

            well, i was just going in to keep jan
            company ... and they ended up telling me
            i needed a special treatment on my hair.
            so...
            suddenly, i was having my hair shampooed
            and wrapped in a towel.
            four hours later, we staggered out
            of the beauty shop.
            they had charged us $60 altogether...
            and i tipped everyone for both of us, and
            jan didn't know ... she tipped them, too.

            our hair looked FAR from desirable.
            in fact, it was perfectly tragic.
            we looked at each other as we crawled into
            the car, and suddenly burst out laughing.

104   laughing
because that's better than crying.
   because NOTHING is so terrible as to
   become bitter and angry and hostile.
     that only makes it worse.
   there are so many things
   more shattering than a bad do at
   the beauty shop.
   smile.

two weeks ago, in chicago's o'hare airport, i was
dragging from one terminal to another,
with all my "paraphernalia" ...
hot and exhausted and ready to drop
one of the bags ANYTIME.
a friend was with me, and
suddenly, i threw everything i had
on the floor.
dozens of people were racing by me.
they stopped and stared a moment, while
   i stood there crying.
     ANGRY ... that's what i felt!

   it was disgusting to try to conquer
     that unbearable airport.
       then, i laughed.

i laughed because it must have looked
so ridiculous to be standing there in the middle
of that hectic, enormous place...
   with my bags everywhere,
     crying.

     picking everything up, i stumbled to

a row of seats, put everything down...
and went to the chocolate shop.

it didn't matter whether i would get fat
or not ... i ordered a whole sack of
candy and sat down and ate it ALL
before i proceeded to the next gate.

humor made the DIFFERENCE.
it gave me survival.

have you ever bought a dress or a pair of pants
and hurried home to get ready for a big night's event?
i know a couple who did...
except they both noticed their clothes
were too long.
rather than become furious, frantic,
and uptight ... they laughed,
and the wife found a roll of masking tape
and proceeded to tape up her husband's
trousers
and her dress.
they went to the banquet,
no one knew...
they enjoyed the evening without
guilt feelings for getting angry...
they wore a secret smile about
masking tape no one saw.

one family i know struggles financially.
when i went to dinner one night, i noticed the
table was elegantly set
with candlelight and fine bone china
and linen napkins.

the buzzers on the oven kept going off, and
i wondered what exquisite gourmet thing we
would be getting for our main course.

when i was called to the table, the wife brought
out a fancy platter with hamburgers on it.
yep ... that's what we had.
hamburgers and potato salad
on fine china.
    they said it was so much easier to
    toss their heads back and laugh about insufficient
        funds ... and put
            color into the meal...
                than to cry.

i really believe the happy people...
    people we all like being around...
        those who conquer good over evil,
those are the people
who have learned to laugh
easily ... to find humor...
    who never allow satan the advantage
        of dragging their spirits to the ground.
    of thinking he's the winner.

a merry heart doeth good....

riding the rapids

107   i'm at a camp in colorado.
it's for youth-for-Christ teens from
    several states.

today, i decided to ride the rapids
with a group of kids.
    for an hour, in a bus packed with three
        to a seat, we wound up narrow mountain roads
to a turbulent, raging piece
    of river.

we would go down the rapids two at a time,
    in small, air-blown rafts. one of the staff
and i decided to team up, and started out.

at the end of our run, there would be men
with a rope pulled across the width of the river
to catch us
    so we wouldn't be carried for miles
        down more dangerous rapids.

there were some rough spots,
    strong undertows and whirlpools, where, if your
        raft got caught, you would spin and be unable to
            pull out.

today, if never before, no one could call any of us
gutless ... never had i done ANYTHING that took
more courage
        than heading down that pounding, racing
        water with nothing but an oar to hang onto,
    and my legs dangling over the side.

a couple of rafts had gone ahead of us, and i had

108   watched them hit strong currents. the people were
thrown recklessly into the water—and
        dragged under the surface for a
            terrifyingly long stretch.

faye and i seemed to be doing well. our raft was
steady, and we kept to the left
        of the river, which was the smoothest side.
            we flew over huge rocks, and down into
                turbulence, but we hung on, still
in the raft.

as we neared the roughest spot of all, i was terrified. i
resigned myself to the fact that i'd be thrown out, and
i must brave the results.
        God and blessing were with us as we seemed
            to hit the big drop right in the center,
                between the fierce undertow and the
                    whirlpool.
we flew down the descending rapids between large
boulders, and when we discovered that we had
conquered the roughest spot with success, we began
to laugh and scream for
        all the onlookers high above...
        "we did it ... WE DID IT ... Yahoooooooo."

well...
where the rope was supposed to be, there was none.
the men didn't realize we were that close, and were
unprepared for us. as we raced past them, one small
man leaped out, grabbed onto our raft, and hung on
fiercely.

    we were swept down the river with no ability

109   whatsoever to stop ourselves ... or direct the raft
       to shore.

       over huge rocks, down steep declines ... we
       raced. ed was hanging on desperately, wanting
       to save us. almost oblivious to his legs being
       bashed against the rocks, he hung on.

       suddenly, we could see we were approaching a deep
       drop-off over a large rock. i was at the front of the
       raft. ed, by this time, had thrown himself between
       faye and me. as we flew over the rock,
           i was flung under the swirling water and
              carried across the rocks and down
                 the river.

       i remember looking back and seeing faye and ed so
       far behind me, on the raft, hanging onto some
       branches.
           the river dragged me farther and farther away.
              some of the kids were running along the bank,
                 trying to keep up with me, and screaming...
       but they couldn't help either.

       i tried to scream, but my head was so full of water i
       could hardly breathe. there was no one ahead to catch
       me. i wondered when i would be thrown against
       another big rock.
           for the first time in my life, death was vivid and
           real, and i cried to God for mercy.

       several weeks before, i had heard someone say, "water
       won't kill you if you relax, so don't fight it."

110   i tried to take deep breaths ... to relax as the raging
       water tossed me around.

       suddenly, james, one of the high school boys, threw
       himself into the water and stretched his arm as far as
       he could, and i grabbed it ... and
           another boy grabbed him
               from shore.

       ed, with blood streaming down his shins, ran up and
       hugged and kissed me. he didn't know his legs were
       bruised and injured. i was safe, and he was thanking
       God and crying.

           now it's late.
           i've had dinner, spoken to the kids, and
           all several hundred of them are bunked down in
               cabins for the night.

       crawling into bed, i've cried out all my
       terror for the first time.

       a river of that force and power...
           of that magnitude and mystery...
       who could question the greatness of God...
           His authorship?
       what human being would dare to make
       himself or herself master of life?

       "what is man, that Thou art mindful of him?"

       you know, God...
           without You, i'd live scared.

psalm 63

oh, God, You are my Father ... each morning
   i'll seek Your face ... my soul
cries out for your mercy ... i long for a
   touch of your grace...

though it seems i'm often surrounded
   by a dry and terrible land ... i behold
your power and glory ... and i know that i'm
   safe in your hand...

your love is better than life ... and my
   heart longs to offer you praise ... so i'll
lift up my hands and i'll worship You ... and
   be satisfied all
     of my days.

when i make my bed in the darkness,
   i will sing with joy a new song ... and
     recall all the times that you've
rescued me ... and i'll worship You
   all my life long.

(skillings, *celebration of hope*)

small things

113   how incredible
that one of my greatest blessings came
from an invitation to a small
church in florida.
God often turns the smallest moment into
the greatest tomorrows of potential.

the pastor wasn't famous.
the building was small and plain.
BUT Jesus knew a secret.

it was so hard for me to fly that friday after being
dean of women all week...
    knowing that i would return on sunday to be
    dean all the next week. i was so busy ... but i had
    promised to go.

it happened that a lady was visiting her sister in that
florida city, and decided to come hear me tell my
dreams.

dot mccollister went back to baton rouge, louisiana,
and decided i should come to HER neighborhood.
not only did her neighbors bring much love and
blessing into my life, and share my dreams for
THEIR world—but dot and her husband, rolfe,
became a family who have taught me a lot.

from that unnoticed weekend in florida, rolfe and
some of his friends introduced me to a committee in
washington, d.c., and i was invited to speak at the
national bicentennial luncheon...
    and then the one in san bernardino, california...
    and lincoln, nebraska ... and waterloo, iowa.

114   don't wait for the BIG moments.
        pour yourself into the small, obscure ones.
            they determine where your heart really is.
            they give Jesus room to surprise you.
                you'll see.
        i've learned it over and over.

        there's something i want you to know about
        rolfe mccollister ... he is BRAVE!

        i've heard him pray...
        "Jesus, make me YOUR man.
            whatever it takes, use me.
            you know my biggest problem is my ego...."
        that takes courage.
        that means he desires to be God's person more
        than he wants security and financial success and
        health and acceptance.

        one time, while i was visiting in baton rouge, rolfe
        had his wife host a tea for all the wives of his law
        partners and the bank board. he asked me to speak
        to them. i was SCARED because those women were
        so sophisticated and polished. i blew in with a
        simple smock dress and sandals. rolfe was there to
        introduce me. whispering a prayer for boldness (i
        think i wouldn't have been so frightened if they
        had been men), i started....

        "Jesus is Lord of my life.
        He laughs with me and cries with me
            and helps me climb my mountains ... and
        well ... could i sing you a little song?"

they listened.
        it wasn't just a tea.
        it was a tea in HIS Name.
            i admired rolfe for being man enough
                to host it.

        this one family has put so much color and blessing
        and love and belonging into my life,
            and my family's.
        Jesus has used them to make up to me
        all the cold airports and lonely hotel rooms.
            sometimes, when the world seems so big
                and i feel pretty small, i love knowing there
                    is a man like rolfe in the world who is
                        unashamed
        to be a real Christian,
            to carry booklets in his shirt pocket that
                he can use to share Christ in his law practice.

        it all started
        in a little church
        in an obscure city
        in florida.

        tonight i was wondering exactly where billy graham
        found Jesus ... and if it was an unexpected experience
        in a small unnoticed place....

        i'll bet the nurse who first bathed and diapered harry
        truman never realized that her care would some day
        contribute to the making of a president.

        today,
        where you are,

116   in a silly, minuscule experience,
       you may touch someone who will some day
       touch someone who eventually
       will touch a Christian leader of
       tomorrow.

       so don't be surprised....

me and my neighborhood

117   for me, there's just Jesus and people.
       right here.
       now.
       where i live.

       not how much money i'll have
           when i'm 60...
           or how many best-selling books...
           or where i've traveled.
       just Jesus and people and me.

       that's why i want to tell you about my
       neighborhood...
           that's my world.
           it's boston.

       the zigelbaums.
       he's a jewish psychiatrist.
       they live across the street.
           hal and susie, their children,
           were on the cover and
           inside pages of my last book,
           i love the word impossible.

       those children flew with me to chicago.
       for one day, in 95 degree heat.
       we climbed the jungle gym
           and rode the swings and teeter-totter
               and merry-go-round...
       and they snapped pictures.
       then we returned
       to *tyndale* where dr. taylor scooped up those two
           children in his arms, and asked them their favorite
           colors. susie's was hot pink; hal's was purple.

do you know
dr. taylor went SOMEWHERE and
found hot pink and purple children's Bibles for them!

we flew home that night, and dr. and mrs. zigelbaum
hugged the children, and we took them home and
tucked them in bed.

"ann ... for you to take the children today...
    to want them in the book...
        you have crystallized love for us in a
            way it hasn't been crystallized before.
        can Jesus live in us the way He does you?"

yes.
He lives for EVERYONE.
and last week, over thanksgiving, ziggy and patti
    (that's what you can call them
    if you ever meet them in boston)
    flew with me
        to boise, idaho, where i spoke at northwest
            nazarene college.
on a thanksgiving evening,
with several thousand people,
we were ONE.
hundreds of Christians, and
    dr. and mrs. zigelbaum.
    we cried together,
        and laughed
        and shared dreams
    and reached out for warm, strong handshakes.
    love swept across the gymnasium,
    and we'll never be the same.

farmers and home folks and
professors and college students
and children and grandparents....

i was there with a piece
of my world.
alleluia.

jimmy works in the parking booth where i live.
if you are coming to shop, you have to pay
   to park there. he's my friend.
      he volunteers to wax my car...
         just because.

well, one night i pulled through the drive, and
jimmy flagged me down....

"park HERE ... i brought wax in my trunk ... i'll wax
   your car in between checking all the other cars
      in and out...."

TERRIFIC!

thirty minutes later i came down.
he was working hard.

"jimmy, what can i do to thank you?"

"we could have a can of beer together in your
   apartment."

i don't know what i expected him to say,
but i didn't expect THAT.

but
in my mind
i remembered all the times
i wanted to share Jesus with jimmy.
   there were always
   cars and sirens and horns and people.

Jesus,
you don't care about jimmy's beer ... do you?
You care about JIMMY.

"jimmy, where's your beer?"

"in the parking booth..."

i was raised in a strict, evangelical home.
i had never touched a can of beer.
walking over to the booth, i reached in and pulled
   out this can of beer
      and hid it in my trenchcoat so no one
         would see, and told jimmy to come up when
         he was finished.

Jesus, i hope this is YOUR idea.
help me.

jimmy came.
i set his can of beer on one side,
and poured myself ginger ale.

"jimmy, the car looks great.
   THANKS.

for ever so long, i've wanted to tell
                    you the most exciting thing in my life...."

"what's that?"

"Jesus. He's the Lord of my life.
    He loved me when i couldn't love myself
        and has forgiven me when no one else has
            wanted to
        and i couldn't forgive myself.
He's love ... and jimmy, love changes
EVERYTHING."

"ann, can ANYONE know Jesus like that?"

anyone can.
anywhere.
Jesus is love, and love is
    like that.
    always.

you say,
"ann, why didn't you make jimmy drink
    ginger ale with you,
    instead of letting him have his beer?"

i don't know.
i guess because i think Jesus would have taken
him right where he lived....
what really mattered to Jesus
    was that jimmy know He was love.
        that He cared.
Jesus and jimmy have years to work on
the details of jimmy's life.

122　　that night,
　　　in one, small, simple way
　　　i felt i had moved the world.
　　　　an everyday person
　　　right where i live.
　　　i reminded jimmy that Jesus IS alive,
　　　and He is love.
　　　that makes ALL the difference.

　　　kristin lives across the street.
　　　she is nine.
　　　her mother is a beautiful woman who edits
　　　the waterfront paper. her father is a jewish
　　　attorney.

　　　our life-styles and perspectives
　　　are probably very different in many ways,
　　　but we are friends.

　　　one night, late, i ran over with
　　　a little tiny hanging for kristin's wall.
　　　　just to celebrate our friendship.
　　　　　because i think she is special.
　　　i hugged her tight,
　　　and read a little story she wrote,
　　　and watched her nine-year-old flair.

　　　"kristin ... listen to this little song...
　　　　'God loves you and i love you
　　　　　and that's the way it should be...'
　　　that is from me to you.
　　　when you grow up, always remember."

　　　we laughed.

123   i had tea with her dad and mom.
            an ordinary night.
                in the heart of boston.

        they let me talk about Jesus.
        i let them be themselves.
        isn't that God's idea of belonging!

        "o Jesus, boston is so big,
        and i am just one ... but help me to be what
        you would be if you lived here in person."

            every day, if mario and lenny are vacuuming the
            hall on MY floor, i run outside my apartment just
            to thank them. in the mornings, i run down to greet
            the postman, rick, because he does such a special job
        of sorting through all my mail,
                and it's A LOT.
                he never complains.
                always, there is a warm smile.

        carol is a beauty shop operator.
        she is catholic. i am protestant.
        we pray together
            and eat good food
                and she often brings me
        fresh flowers for my table.
        Jesus has come to both of us
        right here in my little living room.

        frank and joe and mike and tony...
        they take care of my building.
        the shrubs and halls and windows and leaks.

124   one day, i tried to find tony because i was
flying somewhere to speak, and i wanted to tell
him goodbye...
    that no matter where i go,
i pray for him every day.

finally, after looking EVERYWHERE, i discovered
him in the delicatessen shop
eating an egg salad sandwich.

"tony, i wanted to tell you goodbye.
i'll be gone a few days ... but
    wherever i am, i'll be praying for you.
       i love you, and Jesus does, and never forget."

"oh, ann, don't pray for me...
    i'm going down there" (and he pointed way
      DOWN) "with everyone else...."

    "oh, no you aren't ... i pray for you ... that makes
    a difference."

i hugged him, and knocked his egg salad sandwich
on the floor, and we both felt terrible ... but
before i crawled into the cab, tony yelled,

"ann, thanks. i'll remember."

tony is special.
he has dignity and value in the world.
Jesus can use him.
you'll see.

you know what?

125   now tony says he prays for me, too!
smile.

there are so many i wish you could meet.
natalie runs the little book shop on the first floor,
    and paula the dress shop. emma is a professor.
    milo and jim are guards in the lobby. they even
    water my plants
    when i'm out of town.
    jerry owns a big hotel in boston.

joel is another jewish attorney
who is one of my very special people. he
lets me eat lunch with him and his business friends.
i sing them little songs, and pray for our food.

joel says,
"oh, ann, you really believe, don't you?"

"i do."

my back is straight.
my head high.
a giant of a God lives in me.
i'm not scared.

last week, i had my first
little Bible study in my
apartment. six women.
    some of them had never even prayed
    out loud before—you could tell.
    hot tea and coffee cake and Jesus and us.
        "it only takes a spark to get
            a fire going...."

126   it's not what people do...
        where they go
            how different their opinions are from mine.
               if they are Christian or not.
it's what ANN is.

oh, i always want to wear a smile
reach out for a strong handshake
and look people square in the eye.
to laugh easily.
    listen carefully.
        meet people's needs
        right where they are...
            in Christ's Name.

i want to keep wrapping my arms around the world,
and loving them.
    where they hurt.
    in ways that count.
    as Jesus would do.

Jesus and people and me.
that's all.